The Georgics of Virgil

By

Publius Vergilius Maro

Translated from the Latin by

J. W. MacKail

First published in 1934

Published by Left of Brain Books

Copyright © 2023 Left of Brain Books

ISBN 978-1-397-66630-7

First Edition

All rights reserved. No part of this publication may be reproduced, distributed, or transmitted in any form or by any means, including photocopying, recording, or other electronic or mechanical methods, without the prior written permission of the publisher, except in the case of brief quotations permitted by copyright law. Left of Brain Books is a division of Left Of Brain Onboarding Pty Ltd.

PUBLISHER'S PREFACE

About the Book

"The Georgics, the second major poem which Virgil composed, took seven years to write. He finished it in 29 B.C.E.; it was read to Augustus on his return from the east. This work consists of two thousand lines of poetry on the subject of agriculture, with patriotic overtones and rich mythological allusions. Although some consider this Virgils' best work, the poet was never completely satisfied with it, as he immediately started work on the Aeneid and never returned to it. Virgil requested on his deathbed that the Georgics be supressed; Augustus, however, intervened."

(Quote from sacred-texts.com)

CONTENTS

PUBLISHER'S PREFACE
  BOOK FIRST 1
  BOOK SECOND 16
  BOOK THIRD 32
  BOOK FOURTH 48

BOOK FIRST

WHAT makes the cornfields glad; beneath what star it befits to upturn the ground, Maecenas, and clasp the vine to her elm; the tending of oxen and the charge of the keeper of a flock; and all the skill of thrifty bees; of this will I begin to sing. You, O bright splendours of the world, who lead on the rolling year through heaven; Liber and gracious Ceres, if by your gift Earth exchanged Chaonian acorns for the swelling ear, and tempered her draughts of Achelous with the discovered grape; and you, O Fauns, guardian presences of the country, trip it together, Fauns and Dryad girls; of your gifts I sing. And thou, Neptune, at whose mighty trident-stroke Earth first bore the neighing steed; and thou, O forester, whose three hundred snow-white bullocks crop the rich Cean brakes; even thou, leaving thy native woodland and thy Lycean lawns, Pan of Tegea, shepherd of the flock, so thou love thy Maenalus, be gracious and come; and Minerva inventress of the olive, and thou, boy teacher of the crooked plough, and Silvanus carrying thy slim cypress uprooted; gods and goddesses all who keep the fields in your care, or who feed the fresh plants from no sown seed, or who send down on the crops plentiful rain from heaven; and thou, whatsoever place thou art soon to hold in the gods' consistory, whether thou wilt look on cities and have earth in keeping, and the vast world receive thee as fosterer of harvests and sovereign of seasons, and wreathe thy brows with thy mother's myrtle; or whether thou come as god of the infinite sea, and thy deity only be adored of sailors, to thee utmost Thule be tributary, thy hand Tethys purchase for her daughter with dower of all her waves; or whether thou set thyself as a new sign among the lingering months, where space opens between Erigone and the following Claws, while before thee the blazing Scorpion draws in his arms, and retreats from more than the allotted space of heaven; whatso thou wilt be-- for neither does hell hope thy reign, nor may so dread a desire of reigning ever be thine, though Greece be enrapt in her Elysian plains, and Proserpine care not to follow the mother who calls her back: grant a fair passage, and favour my bold endeavour, and with me pitying the country folk who know not of the way, advance, and even now learn to be called on in prayer.

In early spring, when chilly moisture trickles from the hoar hills and the crumbling clod thaws in the west wind, even then would I have the bull begin to groan over the deep-driven plough and the share glitter with polish of the furrow. That field at last replies to the greedy farmer's prayers, which has twice felt the sun, twice the frost; that bursts his granaries with overflowing harvests.

And ere yet our iron cleaves the unknown plain, be our care first to learn the winds, and the sky's shifting mood, and the ground's native nurture and dress, and what each quarter will bear and what each will reject. Here corn, there grapes come more prosperously; yonder the tree drops her seedlings, and unbidden grasses kindle into green. Seest thou not how Tmolus sends scent of saffron, India ivory, the soft Sabaeans their spice; but the naked Chalybes steel, and Pontus the castor drug, Epirus mares for Elean palms? From of old Nature laid such laws upon certain regions, an everlasting covenant, what time Deucalion of old cast on the unpeopled globe those stones whence the hard race of man was born. Come therefore, from the first months of the year straightway let the strong bulls upturn the rich floor of earth, and the full strength of summer suns bake the flat clods to dust. But if the land be not fertile, it will serve to ridge it by shallow furrows hard on Arcturus' rising; there, lest weeds choke the corn's luxuriance; here, lest scant moisture leave a barren waste of sand.

In turn likewise shalt thou let the stubbles lie fallow, and the idle field crust over unstirred; or else there under changed skies sow golden spelt, where before thou hadst reaped the pea with wealth of rattling pods, or the tiny vetch crop, or the brittle stalks and rustling underwood of the bitter lupin. For the field is drained by flax-harvest and wheat-harvest, drained by the slumber-steeped poppy of Lethe, but yet rotation lightens the labour; only scorn not to soak the dry soil with fattening dung, nor to scatter grimy ashes over the exhausted lands. Thus too the fields find rest in change of crop; nor meanwhile are thanks lost on unploughed land. Often likewise it is well to burn barren fields and consume the light stubble in crackling flame: whether that earth thence conceives secret strength and sustenance, or all her evil is melted away and her useless moisture sweats out in the fire; or that the heat opens more of these ducts and blind pores that carry her juices to the fresh herbage; or rather hardens and binds her gaping veins against fine rain or the fierce sun's mastery or the frostbite of the searching North.

Great service withal he does the fields who breaks their dull clods with the mattock and drags osier hurdles over them, nor from high Olympus does golden Ceres regard him in vain; or he who, raising ridges along the furrowed plain, again turns his plough to break them across, and labours earth incessantly and makes the fields own his sway.

Pray for dripping midsummers and clear winters, O husbandmen; from winter dust the spelt grows strongest, and the field is glad; never does Mysia triumph in such pride of tillage, or Gargarus himself wonder at his harvests. Why tell of him, who, when the seed is cast, follows close over the field and breaks down the lumps of sticky soil? then guides over the crops chasing runlets from the river; and when the blade is dying on the scorched and feverous field, look! on the brow of the slope he lures the wave from her channel; the falling wave wakens a hoarse chatter among the smooth pebbles, and gushes cool over the parched fields. Why of him, who, lest the stalk sink prone under the heavy car, grazes down the rankness of the cornfield in the tender blade, when the crop first levels the furrow? or who gathers and drains away the moisture of the marsh with porous gravel, above all if in the doubtful months the floods go out on the river, covering all the broad flats with mud, and leave pools steaming with warm moisture in the hollows.

Nor yet, though labours of men and oxen have so wrought in turning the soil, are the villain goose and Strymonian crane and the bitter-fibred succory unavailing to injure, or the shade to harm. Our Lord himself willed the way of tillage to be hard, and long ago set art to stir the fields, sharpening the wits of man with care, nor suffered his realm to slumber in heavy torpor. Before Jove no tillers made the fields subject; not even might the plain be parted by landmark or boundary line; men gathered to a common store, and unaided and unasked earth bore all things in a fuller plenty. He it was who gave the black snake his venom, and bade wolves ravin and the sea be tossed, who shook the honey from the leaves and took fire away, and stopped the brooks that ran wandering with wine: that so practice and pondering might slowly forge out many an art, might seek the corn-blade in the furrow and strike hidden fire from the veins of flint. Then first rivers felt the hollowed alder, then the sailor gave the stars their number and name, Pleiads and Hyades and the bright Lycaonian Bear. Then was invented the snare to catch game and the treacherous lime-twig, and the ring of dogs round the wide forest-lawn; and even now one whips the wide stream and searches the pool with his casting-net, and another draws his lines dripping from the sea. Then rigid iron and the blade of the shrill saw came--for they of old split wood in clefts with wedges--then arts many in sort; nothing but yielded to unrelenting toil and the hard pressure of poverty. Ceres first instructed mortals to upturn earth with iron, when now acorns and arbute-berries were failing from the sacred forest, and Dodona denied them sustenance. Soon the labour of the cornfield too increased; vile mildew must devour the stalk and the thistle lift over the field his lazy spears: the crop dwindles, a rough forest of clivers and burs advances, and fruitless darnel and barren wild-oats reign over the shining tilth. Nay, except thou wilt harass the weeds with ceaseless mattock, and frighten off the birds with clamour, and thy pruning-hook lop the darkening rustic shades and thy prayers call down the rain, ah! all in vain wilt thou eye the garner pile of another, and allay thine own hunger from the shaken oak in the woodland.

Likewise must be told what are the weapons of the hardy countryfolk, without which can be neither sowing nor springing of harvests: the share first, and the heavy strength of the curved plough, and the slow rolling wagons of our Lady of Eleusis, sledges and harrows and the weary weight of the mattock; withal the slight wicker ware of Celeus, arbutus hurdles, and Iacchus' mystical winnowing-fan. All these thou wilt heedfully provide and lay up long in store, if the divine country keeps her due honour in thine eyes. Early the forest elm is bowed by main force to bend into a share-beam, and takes the shape of the curving plough; to the stock of it are fitted the long eight-foot pole, the two mould-boards, and the double back of the share-head; and the light lime is cut to season for the yoke, and the tall beech for the plough-tail that is to turn the carriage from above and behind, and oak battens are hung over the fire for the smoke to search them through.

I can repeat to thee many a counsel of them of old, if thou shrink not back nor weary to learn of lowly cares. Above all must the threshing-floor be levelled with the ponderous roller, and wrought by hand and cemented with clinging potter's clay, that it may not gather weeds nor crack in the reign of dust, and be playground withal for manifold destroyers. Often the tiny mouse builds his house and makes his granaries underground, or the eyeless mole scoops his cell; and in chinks is found the toad, and all the swarming vermin that are bred in earth; and the weevil, and the ant that fears a destitute old age, plunder the great pile of spelt.

Look thou likewise, when the walnut in the woodland attires herself in wealth of blossom, and bends with scented boughs; if her fruit exceed, the corn will keep pace with it, and abundant threshing come with abundant beat; but if her shade overflow in luxuriance of leaf, vainly will the chaff-laden straw be beaten on the winnowing-floor.

In truth I have seen many a sower steep his seeds and wash them beforehand in black olive-lees, that the fruit in the treacherous pod might be larger and soften quickly even over a little fire: I have seen them, though long chosen and toilsomely approved, still fall off unless the strong hand of man picked the largest year by year: so it is fated that all things run to the worse and fall dropping backwards; even as one who with strain of oarage urges a skiff up stream, if once he slacken his arms, the prone river current sweeps him headlong down.

Likewise must we no less regard the star of Arcturus and the days of the Kids and the gleaming Serpent, than they who sailing homeward over windswept seas adventure the Pontic and the straits by Abydus' oyster-beds. When the Scales make daylight and sleep equal in hours and just halve the globe between light and shadow, set your bulls at work, O men! sow the barley-fields, right into the showery skirts of frost-bound mid-winter: no less is it time to cover in earth the flax-plant and the corn-poppy, and to urge on the belated ploughs while the dry soil allows it, while the clouds hang aloft. In spring beans are sown; then the crumbling furrows receive thee likewise, clover of Media, and the yearly care of the millet crop approaches; when the milk-white Bull with gilded horns opens the year, and the setting Dogstar retires backwards. But if for wheaten harvest or strong spelt thou wilt work thy ground, and the corn-ear alone is thy desire, first let the Atlantides be at their morning setting and the blazing star of the Cretan Crown sink away, ere thou yield their debt of seed to the furrows, or ere thou hasten to intrust the year's hope to an unwilling earth. Many begin before the setting of Maia; but a harvest of empty stalks mocks their expectation. If indeed thou wilt sow the vetch or the common kidney-bean, nor despite the care of the Pelusiac lentil, the setting Bear-warden will send thee no uncertain sign; begin, and carry thy sowing on to the mid-frost.

To this end the golden sun rules an orbit measured out in certain divisions through the twelvefold star-girdle of the world. Five zones are placed in heaven; whereof one ever reddens in the blazing sun and ever is parched by his fire; and round it right and left sweep the utmost two, bleak, stiff in ice and dark with showers; two between these and the central zone are granted by grace of the gods to weary mortals, and through both a path is drawn where the slant procession of the signs may turn. The world, rising steeply towards Scythia and the Rhipean fortresses, sinks sloping to Libya and the south. This pole of ours is ever uplifted; but the other black Styx and the deep world of ghosts see underneath their feet. Here the enormous Serpent glides forth, wreathing his coils in fashion of a river around and between the two Bears, the Bears that dare not dip under the Ocean floor: there, one saith, either dead night is soundless, and the gloom thickens in night's perpetual pall, or dawn returns from us and leads back the day; and when dayspring touches us with his panting horses' breath, there crimson Hesperus kindles his lamp at evenfall. Hence can we foreknow the changeful sky's seasons, hence the day of harvest and the time of sowing, and when it befits to drive our oars through the treacherous sparkling sea, when to launch armed fleets, or in due season lay low the woodland pine.

Neither in vain do we mark the signs in their dawning and decease, and the four seasons that make equal division of the year. Whensoever chilly rain keeps the husbandman indoors, many a thing, which must else be hurried through in clear weather afterward, may be done at leisure; the ploughman beats out the stubborn point of his blunted share; one hollows troughs out of the tree; one marks the stamp on the flock or the numbers on the grain-sacks; others sharpen stakes and forked poles, and sort Amerian bands for the trailing vine. Now let the basket be lightly woven of briar-rods, now parch corn over the fire and pound it in the stone. Nay, and even on holydays some works are right and lawful; no scruple forbids to guide forth the rivulet, to fence off the cornfield, to set snares for birds, to burn brambles, and to plunge the bleating flock in the healthful stream: often the driver loads his slow-paced donkey's sides with oil or cheap apples, and returning, carries a dressed mill-stone or a lump of black pitch back with him from the town.

The moon's self ordains the days in their several order to be diverse in luck of labour. Shun the fifth, birthday of pale Orcus and the Eumenides; on it earth bore that accursed brood, Coeus and Iapetus and fell Typhoeus, and the brothers that leagued to pluck down heaven. Thrice they essayed to plant Ossa on Pelion, ay, and roll up leafy Olympus upon Ossa: thrice our Lord smote asunder the piled mountains with his thunderbolt. The seventeenth is lucky for setting the vine, for catching and breaking oxen, for stringing loops in the loom: the ninth favours runaways, but thwarts the thief.

Many a thing even makes better way in the chill of night, or when at sundawn earth is dewy under the orient star. By night the light stubbles, by night the parched meadows are better mown; clinging moisture fails not through the night. And one I know keeps awake late by the winter firelight, and points torchwood with sharp steel: meanwhile, lightening her long toil with song, the wife runs her ringing comb through the web, or boils down the sweet liquid must over the fire and skims with leaves the wave of the bubbling copper. But ruddy corn is cut in noon-day heat, and in noon-day heat the parched grain is trodden on the threshing-floor.

Strip to plough, strip to sow; winter is the farmer's holiday, and the husbandmen feast on their stores all through the frozen time, and spread the banquet among themselves in mirthful round. Merry winter bids the guest and lightens the heart; even as when laden keels at last touch their haven, and the rejoicing mariners hang garlands on the stern. But then nevertheless is the season to strip acorns from the oak and berries of the laurel, the olive and the blood-red myrtle: then to set snares for the crane and nets for the stag, and to hunt the long-eared hare; then to strike down the fallow-deer with the whirling stroke of the hempen Balearic sling, while snow lies deep, while ice blocks the rivers.

Why tell of autumnal storms and stars, and when now the day is briefer and the summer softer, what watches men must keep? or when showerful spring pours down, when the spiky harvest even now ripples on the plains, and when the green blade swells with her milky grain? Often have I seen, when the husbandman was marching in his reapers to the golden fields and just cutting the slim-stalked barley, how all the winds, clashing in battle, would tear right from the roots and fling high whole breadths of heavy corn; in so black a gust would the storm sweep light blade and flying straw away. Often likewise the waters of heaven descend in infinite armies, and clouds charged from the deep thicken into foul weather black with thundershowers: the sky pours sheer down and washes away the glad crops and labours of the oxen with flooding rain; ditches fill, and river channels swell roaring, and the narrow seas seethe and smoke. Our Lord himself in the midnight of the storm-clouds wields the flashing bolts in his right hand: at their shock ancient Earth trembles, wild beasts slink away, and mortal hearts throughout the nations bow low in terror: he hurls down his flaming shaft on Athos or Rhodope or the Ceraunian heights; the south winds blow fiercer and the rain streams drenching down, and the rushing wind wails over forest and shore.

Fearing this, regard thou heaven in his months and seasons, whither the chill star of Saturn withdraws, to what circles in the sky the Cyllenian wanderer turns his fire. Above all, worship thou the gods, and bring great Ceres her yearly offerings, doing sacrifice on the springing grass close on the verge of dying winter, when now spring skies are clear. Then lambs are fat, and then wines mellowest, then sleep is sweet where the shade thickens on the hill. To Ceres let all thy rustic folk do service; to her wash thou the honeycomb with milk and soft wine, and for luck let the victim thrice encircle the springing crops and all the band of thy fellows keep it joyful company, and loudly call Ceres into the homestead: neither let any lay sickle to the ripe ears till in Ceres' praise, his brows wreathed with twisted oak, he move in rude dances and chant her hymn.

And these things that we might avail to learn by sure tokens, the heats and the rains and the winds that bring cold weather, our Lord himself hath ordained what the moon in her month should foreshadow, at what sign the south wind should drop, what husbandmen should often mark and keep their cattle nearer the farmyard. Straightway when gales are gathering, either the seaways begin to shudder and heave, and a dry roaring to be heard on the mountain heights, or the far-echoing beaches to stir, and a rustling swell through the woodland. Even in that hour the rude surge spares not the curving bull, when gulls fly swiftly back from mid ocean and press screaming shoreward, or when sea-coot play on dry land, and the heron leaves his home in the marshes and soars high above the mist. Often likewise when a gale is toward wilt thou see shooting stars glide down the sky, and through the darkness of night long trails of flame glimmer in their track: often light chaff and fallen leaves flutter in air, or floating feathers dance on the water's surface. But when it lightens from the fierce northern regions, and when Eurus and Zephyrus thunder through their hall, the whole countryside is afloat with brimming ditches, and every mariner at sea furls his soaking sails. Never is rain on us unwarned: either as it gathers in the valley bottoms the crane soars high in flight before it; or the heifer gazing up into the sky snuffs the breeze with wide-opened nostril, or the shrill swallow darts circling about the pond, and the frogs in the mire intone their old complaint. Often likewise the ant carries forth her eggs from her secret chambers along her narrow trodden path, and a vast rainbow drinks, and leaving their feeding-ground in long column armies of rooks crowd with flapping wings. Then seafowl many in sort, and birds that search the fresh pools round the Asian meadows of Cayster, eagerly splash showers of spray over their shoulders, and thou mayest see them now ducking in the channels, now running up into the waves, and wantoning in their bath with vain desire. Then the villain raven calls full-voiced for rain, and stalks along the dry sand in solitary state. Nor even to girls who ply their spinning nightlong is the storm unknown, while they see the oil sputter, and spongy mould gather on the blazing lamp.

And even thus sunlight after rain and cloudless clearness mayest thou foresee and know by sure tokens. For then neither is the keen edge of the starlight dulled to view, nor does the moon rise flushed by her brother's rays, nor are thin woolly fleeces borne across the sky; neither do kingfishers beloved of Thetis spread their plumage to the sun's warmth upon the shore, nor unclean swine remember to shake out their litter and toss it with their snout. But the mists gather lower down and settle on the flats, and, constant to sunset, the night-owl from the roof-top keeps vainly calling through the dark. Aloft in the liquid sky Nisus is in sight and Scylla pays the debt of that purple hair: wheresoever her pinions cleave the thin air in flight, lo, hostile, fierce, loud-swooping down the wind, Nisus is upon her; where Nisus mounts into the wind, her hurrying pinions cleave the thin air in flight. There, withal rooks repeat three or four times a clear thin-throated cry, and often where they sit aloft, happy in some strange unwonted delight, chatter together among the leaves, glad when rains are over to look to their little brood and darling nests once again; not, to my thinking, that their instinct is divine or their dower of fate a larger foresight into nature: but when the weather veers about and the saturated air shifts, and under dripping skies of the south what was rare but now condenses and what was dense expands, their temper changes its fashion, and other motions stir within their breasts than stirred while the clouds drove on before the wind; hence the birds make such chorus in the fields, and the cattle are glad, and the rooks caw in exultation.

If indeed thou wilt regard the hastening sun and the moon's ordered sequences, never will an hour of the morrow deceive thee, nor wilt thou be taken in the wiles of a cloudless night. When the moon first gathers her returning fires, if she clasp a dark mist in her dim crescent, drenching rain will be in store for husbandman and seafarer; but if a maiden flush suffuse her face, wind is coming: wind always flushes the gold of the moon: while if at her fourth rising (for that is surest of warrant) she travel through the sky with clear sharp-cut horns, both that whole day and those that shall dawn after it till the month be done will be rainless and windless, and sailors preserved will pay their vows on the shore to Glaucus and Panope and Melicertes son of Ino.

The sun likewise, both in his arising and when he sinks into the waves, will issue signs; most sure are the signs that attend the sun, yielded with morning or at the ascending of the stars. When at dayspring he is dappled with spots and sunk in a mist, and his orbed centre retires, mistrust thou of showers; for a gale is bearing hard from seaward, ill-ominous for trees and crops and herds. Either when towards daybreak spreading shafts struggle out between thick clouds, or when Dawn springs pale from Tithonus' saffron bed, alas! weak defence will the vine-tendril be then to the mellow cluster, so heavily the rough hail dances rattling on the roofs. This likewise, when he has run his race and is now sinking from the sky, will be of yet more service to remember; for often we see shifting colours fluctuate on his face; green presages rain, flame-colour east winds; but if spots begin to mingle with fiery red, then wilt thou see all a single riot of wind and storm-clouds; not on such a night at any persuasion would I voyage through the deep or part moorings from land. But if his circle be bright alike when he brings the day and buries the day he brought, vain will be thy terror of rain-clouds, and thou shalt discern the forests weaving in a clear wind from the north.

Lastly, what burden evenfall carries, whence the wind chases clear the clouds, what the dripping South broods over, the sun will signify to thee; who shall dare to call the sun untrue? He likewise often warns of the imminence of dim alarms, of treachery and the gathering of hidden wars; he likewise had pity on Rome at Caesar's decease, when he veiled his shining face in dim rusty red, and an evil age dreaded eternal night. Yet at that season earth too and the plains of sea, and unclean dogs and ominous birds gave presage. How often did we see Etna flooding the Cyclopean fields with the torrent bursting from her furnaces, and rolling forth balls of flame and molten rocks! Germany heard the clash of armour fill the sky; the Alps quaked with unwonted shocks. Moreover a voice was heard of many among silent groves, crying aloud, and phantoms pallid in wonderful wise were seen when night was dim; and cattle spoke, a monstrous thing: rivers stop and earth yawns; and ivory sheds tears of mourning and bronzes sweat in the temples. Eridanus, king of rivers, whirled whole forests away in the wash of his raging eddies, and swept herds and stalls together all across the plains. Neither at that same time did boding filaments ever cease to show themselves in disastrous victims, or blood to ooze from wells, and high cities to echo night-long with howling of wolves. Never elsewhere did more lightnings fall from clear skies, or ghastly comets so often blaze. Therefore a second time Philippi saw Roman lines meet in shock of equal arms, and our lords forbade not that Emathia and the broad plains of Haemus should twice be fattened with our blood. Surely a time too shall come when in those borders the husbandman, as his crooked plough labours the soil, will find spears eaten away with scaling rust, or strike on empty helms with his heavy mattock, and marvel at mighty bones dug up from their tombs. Gods of our fathers, of our country, and thou Romulus, and Vesta, mother who keepest Tuscan Tiber and the Roman Palatine, forbid not at least that this our prince may succour a ruined world! Long enough already has our life-blood recompensed Laomedon's perjury at Troy; long already the heavenly palace, O Caesar, grudges thee to us, and murmurs that thou shouldst care for human triumphs, where right and wrong are confounded, where all these wars cover the world, where wickedness is so manifold and the plough's meed of honour is gone; the fields thicken with weeds, for the tillers are marched away, and bent sickles are forged into the stiff swordblade: here the Euphrates, there Germany heaves with war; neighbouring cities rush into arms one against another over broken laws: the merciless War-God rages through all the world: even as when chariots bursting from their barriers swerve out on the course, and, vainly tugging at the curb, the driver is swept on by his horses, and the car hearkens not to the rein.

BOOK SECOND

THUS far of tillage of the fields and stars in the sky: now of thee, Bacchus, will I sing, and with thee no less of wood. land copses and the slowly waxing olive growth. Hither, lord of the winepress; here all is full of thy bounties, for thee the field flowers, heavy with tendrils of autumn, and the brimming vintage foams; come hither, lord of the winepress, by my side pluck off thy buskins and dye thy bared ankles in the new wine.

First of all, Nature is manifold in the birth of trees. For some with no human urging come at their own will and spread wide by plain and winding river, like the soft osier and tough broom, the poplar, and pale willow-beds with their silvery leafage; and some rise from seed they drop, like the towering chestnuts, and Jove's winter-oak, lordliest of leafage in the woodland, and those oaks that Greece holds oracular. Others, like the elm and cherry, multiply from the root in serried undergrowth; and the tiny bay-tree on Parnassus springs beneath her mother's vast shade. These ways are of Nature's ancient gift; in these wear their green all the tribes of forest and underwood and sacred grove.

Others there are, which experience has found out for itself on the way. One tears suckers from their mother's tender stern and sets them in trenches; one plunges in the soil stocks and cross-cleft billets and sharpened stakes from the core: and some forest trees await the layer's pinned arch and slips alive in their parent earth: others need a root in nowise, and the pruner doubts not to commit the topmost twigs to earth's keeping.

Nay, and from the dry wood of her sawn trunk, wonderful to tell! the olive pushes forth a root. And often we see the boughs of one turn lightly into another's, and the changed pear-tree bear her grafted apples, and plums redden on the stony cornel.

Wherefore come, O husbandmen, learn the proper training of each after their kinds, and soften the wild fruits by your nurture, nor let earth lie idle: good it is to plant Ismarus thick with vines and clothe mighty Taburnus in olive. And be thou nigh, to fulfil at my side the task begun, Maecenas our honour, by just due the chiefest sharer in our fame, and give thy flying sails to the spacious sea. I ask not to embrace it all in these my verses; no, though I had an hundred tongues and an hundred mouths, and my voice were iron: come, and skirt close by the shore's edge. The earth is in hand: I will not keep thee here in mazes and long-drawn preludes of fabulous song.

Plants that rise unbidden into the borders of day are unfruitful indeed, but lusty and strong of growth, for native force is in the soil. Yet even these, if one graft them or transplant them into trenched mould, will outgrow their savagery, and under ceaseless training will soon follow thy call to whatsoever ways thou wilt. Even the barren sucker that springs from the stem's foot will do likewise, if set in rank over a clean plot; now the mother's deep-foliaged boughs overshadow it, and steal the produce of its growth, and stifle its fruitfulness. Once more, the tree that rises from shed seed is slow in coming, and will yield shade to thy children's children on a later day; apples dwindle, forgetting their former savour, and ragged clusters hang for birds to plunder from the vine.

Truth to say, on all must labour be lavished, and all be forced into the furrow and tamed at a great price. But olive-trees answer better in truncheons, vines in layers, myrtles of Paphos in the solid wood; and from slips are born the hardwood hazel and the mighty ash, and the shady tree of Hercules' garland, and the acorns of our lord of Chaonia; in like wise is born the tall palm and the fir that shall look on the perils of the sea: while by grafting the rough arbutus yields the walnut, and barren planes carry sturdy apple-boughs, chestnuts a beech-crop; and the mountain-ash silvers with white pear-blossom, and swine crush acorns beneath the elm.

Nor is there one single way of grafting and of budding. For where the buds push out from amid the bark and burst their delicate sheaths, there, just on the knot, a narrow slit is made; in it they imbed the shoot of an alien tree, and teach it to grow into the wet sapwood. Or again, smooth trunks are cleft open and a way driven deep by wedges into the core, then grafts of the fruit-tree let in; nor long time, and the tree climbs skyward in breadth of prosperous boughs, and marvels in strange leafage and fruits not her own.

Furthermore, not single in kind are either strong elms or willow and lotus, or cypresses of Ida; nor in a single likeness is born the fat olive, the ball and the spindle-shaped, and the pausian with bitter berry, nor apples in Alcinous' orchards; nor does the same twig bear Crustumian and Syrian pears and the heavy wardens. Not the same is the vintage that trails from trees of ours, and that which Lesbos gathers from the branch of Methymna: there are Thasian and there are pale Mareotic vines, these meet for a rich, those for a lighter soil; and the Psithian more serviceable for raisin-wine, and the thin Lagean that in her day will trip the feet and tie the tongue, and the purple and the earlier grape; and in what verse may I tell of thee, O Rhaetian? yet not even so vie thou with Falernian vaults. Likewise there are Aminaean vines, theirs the soundest wine of all, for which the Tmolian and even the royal Phanaean make room; and the lesser Argitis, that none other may rival whether in abundant flow or in lasting through length of years. Let me not pass thee by, O Rhodian, well-beloved of gods and festal boards, and Bumastus with thy swelling clusters. But there is no tale of the manifold kinds or of the names they bear, nor truly were the tale worth reckoning out; whoso will know it, let him choose to learn likewise how many grains of sand eddy in the west wind on the plain of Libya, or to count, when the violent East sweeps down upon the ships, how many waves come shoreward across Ionian seas.

Nor indeed can all soils bear all things. By riversides willows grow, and alders in thick swamps, barren mountain-ashes on rocky hills; on the seashore myrtle thickets flourish best; and the god of the vine loves open slopes as yew trees do the freezing north. Look too, where the ends of the earth obey men's tillage, on the Arabian dwellings of the East and the painted Gelonian; so diverse are the native lands of trees. Alone India bears black ebony, alone the Sabaeans have their rod of spice. Why should I rehearse to thee the scented wood that drips with balm, and the clusters of the evergreen thorn? why those Aethiopian forests silvered with a soft fleece, or how Chinese comb off leaves their delicate down? or the groves which India wears nearing Ocean in the world's utmost recesses, where no arrow-shot can ever win through air up to the tree-top; and truly these tribes are not slack when they handle the quiver. Media bears the sour juices and lingering savour of the citron, than which naught is more sovereign, if ever a cruel step-mother has drugged the cup with mingled herbs and baleful charms, to arrive for succour and expel the black poison from the limbs. The tree is large, and most like a laurel to view, and were a laurel but for the difference of wide-wafted fragrance, the leaves drop not in any wind, the flower clings close as may be; with it the Medes anoint their faces and perfume their breath, and cure the pantings of old age.

But neither those Median forests where earth is richest, nor fair Ganges and Hermus turbid with gold, may vie with the praise of Italy; not Bactra nor Ind, or all Panchaia with her wealth of spicy sands. This land of ours no bulls with fire-breathing nostrils have upturned where the monstrous dragon's teeth were sown, no harvest of men has bristled up with helms and serried spears; but heavy cornfields and Massic Juice of wine fill it all, olives and shining herds hold it in keeping. Hence the war-horse issues stately on the plain; hence thy white flocks, Clitumnus, and the lordly victim bull, often bathed in thy holy stream, lead on Roman triumphs to the gods' temples. Here is perpetual spring and summer in months not her own; twice the cattle breed, twice the apple tree yields her service. But the raging tigress is not there or the fierce lion-brood, nor does monkshood deceive the wretched gatherer, nor the scaly serpent dart in huge coils over the ground or gather so long a train of spires. Add thereto all her illustrious cities and the labours wrought in her, all her towns piled high by men's hands on their sheer rocks, and her rivers that glide beneath immemorial walls. Or shall I tell of the seas that wash above her and below? or her great lakes. thee, lordly Larius, and thee, Benacus, heaving with billows and roar as of the sea? or tell of her harbours, of the barriers set upon the Lucrine and the thunder of the indignant sea where the Julian wave echoes afar in the tideway, and the Tyrrhene surge pours into the channels of Avernus? She it is likewise who unlocks from her veins streams of silver and ore of brass,, and flows with abundant gold: she who rears a valiant race of men, the Marsian and the Sabellian stock, the Ligurian trained in hardship and the Volscian spearmen; she the Decii, the Marii, and the mighty Camilli, the seed of Scipio stern in war, and thee, princely Caesar, who even now victorious in Asia's utmost borders does keep aloof the unwarlike Indian from the towers of Rome. Hail, mighty mother of harvests, O land of Saturn, mighty of men: for thee I tread among the glories and arts of old, and dare to unseal these holy springs, making the song of Ascra echo through the Roman towns.

Now, for a space, of the tempers of the fields, the strength of each, and the colour, and the native power of fruit-bearing. First, stubborn soils and ungracious hills, fields of lean marl and pebbly brushwood, welcome the long-lived olive groves of Pallas; for sign thereof, in this same region the oleaster springs abundant, and strews, the fields with her wild berries. But fat land glad with sweet moisture, and flats thick with herbage and bounteous in richness, such as many a time we may descry in the cup of a mountain valley (for hither streams trickle from the cliff-tops and draw down their rich mud), and the southern upland that feeds the fern, hateful to crooked ploughs; this one day will yield thee vines excelling in strength and flowing with wealth of wine, this is fertile of the grape, this of such juice as we pour in offering from cups of gold, when the sleek Etruscan blows his ivory flute by the altars and we offer the steaming entrails on bulged platters. But he whose desire is rather the keeping of cattle and calves, or the breed of sheep or she-goats that strip the plantations, let him seek the lawns and distances of rich Tarentum, or such a plain as unhappy Mantua lost, where snow-white swans feed in the weedy river: not clear springs nor grass will fail the flocks, and how much soever the cattle crop through the long days, as much the chilly dew of a brief night will restore. Land that is black and rich under the share's pressure, and crumbling-soiled (for this it is that we imitate by ploughing) is always the best for corn: from no other harvest floor shalt thou discern the slow oxen bring thy wagons oftener home: or where the angry ploughman has carted the forest-trees away, and levelled the copses that lay idle many a year, and rooted clean out the birds' ancient homes; they spring skyward from their abandoned nests, but the tangled field gleams behind the driven share. For in truth the starved gravel of the hill-country scarce serves the bees with dwarf spurge and rosemary; and scaling tufa and chalk tunnelled by black-scaled snakes call no other land their like to furnish dainty food and yield winding retreats for serpents. Such land as exhales thin mist and flitting smoke, and drinks in and drains away the wet at will, such as is evergreen in clothing of native grass, and mars not iron with a scurf of salt rust, this will garland thine elms with laughing vines, this is fruitful of oil, this wilt thou prove in tillage gracious to the flock and yielding under the crooked share. Such is the tilth of wealthy Capua and the coast that borders the Vesuvian ridge, and where Clanius encroaches on desolate Acerrae.

Now I will tell in what wise thou mayest know each from each. If thou must know whether it be loose or compact beyond the wont (since the one is good for corn, the other for Bacchus, for the corn-goddess where more compact, where loosest for the wine-god), first shalt thou choose a spot by eye, and bid a pit be sunk deep in the solid ground, and again replace in it all the soil, and level the earth atop with thy feet. If earth is lacking, loose will be the plot and fitter for flocks and gracious vines; but if it refuses to return whence it came, and soil is over when the trenches are full, that land is solid; look for sticky clods and lumpy ridges, and furrow the ground with thy strongest oxen. Salt land moreover, and sour so-called--unfruitful for corn it is and no ploughing softens it, nor does the grape keep her race nor orchard-fruits their name therein--will offer such proof as this: pluck thou down from the smoky rafters close-plaited wicker-baskets and strainers of wine-presses; herein let that evil soil and sweet spring-water be filled and trodden; all the water will be squeezed out, yes, and large drops trickle through the wickerwork; but the savour will give plain token, and its bitterness felt will writhe the taster's displeased face. Again, what land is fat we learn briefly in this wise: when tossed from hand to hand it never crumbles, but grows sticky like pitch on the fingers in the handling. Wet ground nurtures a taller herbage, and the native growth is ranker than is right. Ah, may mine be not thus over-fertile, nor show itself too lusty in the early blade' Heavy soil betrays itself without words by weight, light likewise; thine eyes will at first glance know the black, and the several colour of each. But to search out cruel cold is difficult: only that sometimes pitch-pines and baleful yews are there, or the dark ivy spreads her creepers.

Which things regarded, remember long time first to bake thy land in the sun and cleave the broad hillsides with thy trenches, first to lay bare the upturned clods to the North, ere thou plant in the glad stock of the vine. Fields of crumbling soil are the best; for that winds and icy frosts provide, and the sturdy delver that shakes and stirs the acres. But men who will let nothing escape their vigilance seek out beforehand a bed where the seedling tree may have her early training, like to that whither thereafter it shall be borne and set in the row, lest a sudden change of mother estrange the plant. Nay, and they score on the bark the quarters of the sky, to replace in each as it stood the face whereon it bore the ardours of the South, the back it turned towards the Pole; so strong is the habit of infancy.

Whether hill or flat be the better for thy vine-setting, inquire beforehand. If thou wilt rule thy plots in a rich plain, plant thickly; thickly set, the vine is no less bounteous in bearing; but if on the sloping soil of knolls or on couchant hills, give the ranks larger room; yet no less let every alley where the trees are set be drawn square and true to line: as often in pomp of war, when a legion deploys in long line of cohorts and draws up from column on the open plain, and the ranks are straightened and all the earth surges wide with sparkle of brass, nor yet do they close in grim conflict, but the War-god wanders wavering amid their arms. Let equal space of passage be measured every way;

not merely that the view may regale a vacant mind, but since none otherwise will earth supply equal strength to all, nor clear space be left for the outstretching boughs.

Haply too thou mayest inquire of the cuttings for thy trenches. The vine I would dare to intrust to ever so slender a furrow: the tree is sunk deeper and right into the earth; the winter-oak beyond all, who, as high as her top scales the air skyward, strikes at root as deep to hell: therefore not storms nor blasts nor rains uproot her; she abides unstirred, and outlives many children's children, and sees roll by her many generations of men; and stretching wide to right and left her strong boughs and arms, uprears the mass of her own enfolding shade.

Neither let thy vineyards slope to the setting sun; neither plant hazel among the vines; neither cut the uppermost vine-switches, or tear away the uppermost shoots from the tree (such is their love of earth); neither plant among them stems of wild olive: for often heedless shepherds drop a spark, which hiding stealthily at first under the resinous bark, fastens on the core, and, darting out among the high sprays, roars loudly skyward; thence pursues its way, and reigns victorious over bough and summit, and wraps all the woodland in flame, and, thickening, streams into the sky in a cloud of pitch-black gloom: above all if a storm falls prone on the forest and the wind fans and spreads the fire. Where this is, the trees have no force left at root, nor can they recover when cut away, nor grow green again from under earth as before; the barren and bitter-leaved oleaster only is left.

Nor let any counsellor how wise soever persuade thee to stir the earth when stiffened under the breath of the North. Then winter keeps the country ice-bound, nor though the seed be scattered lets the frozen root fasten in the ground. Best is the setting of vineyards when with the flush of spring comes that snow-white bird abhorred of long snakes, or hard on the first frost of autumn, when the fiery horses of the sun yet touch not winter, and even now summer passes away. Spring aids woodland leaf and forest tree; in spring earth yearns and cries for the life-giving seed. Then the lord omnipotent of Sky descends in fruitful showers into the lap of his laughing consort, and mingling with her mighty body nourishes all her fruits in might. Then pathless copses ring with warbling birds, and at the appointed days the herds renew their loves; the bountiful land breaks into birth, and the fields unbosom to wavering breezes of the West: everywhere delicate moisture overflows, and the grasses dare in safety to trust themselves to spring suns, nor does the vine-tendril fear gathering gales or sleet driven down the sky by the blustering North, but thrusts forth her buds and uncurls all her leaves. None other to my thinking were the days that shone at the first dawn of the rising world, none other the course they kept; spring was then, spring reigned on the broad earth, and the east wind held back his wintry blasts, when the first-born beasts drank the daylight, and the earthen brood of men reared their head on the firm fields, and the wild creatures were let loose in the forests and the stars in heaven. Neither might things so delicate endure this their toil, except such space of calm passed between the cold and the heat, and earth were cradled by an indulgent sky.

For the rest, what plantations soever thou wilt set over thy fields, scatter fatting dung, and hide it heedfully deep in earth; dig in porous stone or rough shells, for through them rains will trickle and thin vapour ascend, and the plants take courage; and before now have some been found who would load them down with a stone or the weight of a massy tile, this their defence against streaming rains, this when the dogstar brings the heat and the fields gape in cracks for thirst.

The seedlings set, it remains again and again to bank the earth up to the stalks, and swing the stiff hoe, or to work the soil beneath the ploughshare's pressure and wheel thy straining oxen between the vineyard-rows: therewithal to fit together light reeds and shafts of peeled rods, and ashen stakes and strong crutches, in whose strength they may learn to climb, and scorn the winds, and climb from story to story high up the elm.

And while the earlier youth of the fresh foliage grows towards maturity, spare their tenderness; and while the glad shoot springs upward and mounts unchecked into the blue, not yet should it feel the edge of the pruning-knife, but the leaves be broken off and thinned with bent fingers. Thereafter, when now they have shot up and their strong stems enringed the elm, then strip their tresses, then lop their arms; till then they shrink under the steel; then at last keep imperious rule and check the trailing branches.

Likewise must hurdles be woven and all the flock fenced in, specially while the leaf is tender and innocent of toil; since besides rude storms and the tyrant sun, buffaloes from the thickets and restless roe-deer make it their playground, sheep and hungry heifers their pasture. Not so deadly to it is the stiffening chill of hoar-frost, or the whole weight of summer brooding on the parched crags, as the flocks with the poison of their hard teeth, and the indented scar left on the bitten stem. For none other crime is the goat slain to Bacchus on all our altars while the antique plays advance upon the stage, since Theseus' people ordained prizes for inventions among the villages and clustering hamlets, and joyfully amid their cups danced on oiled wine-skins in the soft meadows. And Ausonian settlers likewise, the race sent forth from Troy, disport with rude verses and careless jest, and put on frowning masks of hallow cork, and call on thee, O Bacchus, in joyous song, and to thee hang swinging amulets from the lofty pine. Thus all their vines ripen with abundant increase, and teem in hollow dells and deep lawns and wheresoever the god turns his goodly head. Therefore meetly shall we recite Bacchus' due honour in ancestral hymns, and bear cakes and platters, and led by the horn the victim goat shall stand by the altar, and the fat flesh roast on spits of hazelwood.

Likewise is there that other labour of vine-dressing, which nothing is ever enough to satisfy; for year by year must all the soil thrice and again be loosened, and the mattock everlastingly turned to break the clod, must all the orchard be lightened of his leaf. The circling toil of the husbandman returns even as the year rolls back on itself along the familiar track. And now what time the vineyard sheds her lingering leaves and the icy North scatters the tresses of the forest, even then the active farmer reaches his care into the coming year, and presses on to lop the bared vine and trim it into shape with the crooked tooth of Saturn. Be first to dig the ground, first to wheel away and burn the prunings, and first to carry the vine-poles indoors; be last to gather the vintage. Twice the shade thickens on thy vines, twice weeds clothe the field with thick entanglements; both make hard work; praise great estates, farm a little one. And therewithal the rough shoots of broom are cut in the woodland, and the river-reed on the banks, and the wild osier-bed gives work to keep. Now the vines are tied, now the shrubberies lay by the pruning-knife, now the last vine-dresser sings over his finished plots: yet must the soil be broken and the dust stirred, and the lord of the sky be dreaded for the grapes even as they ripen.

Contrariwise olives grow all untended; they look not for the sickle-shaped knife or the stiff hoe, when once they have struck root on the field and borne the weather: earth herself, when laid open by the crooked fang, yields sap in sufficience and heavy crops following the ploughshare: so shalt thou nurture the fat olive dear to Peace.

Orchard-trees likewise, so soon as they feel strength in their stem and possess their full vigour, climb fast skyward of their own force and needing no aid of ours: no less withal the whole woodland grows heavy with increase, and the untilled haunts of birds flush with blood-red berries; the cytisus is mown, the high forest yields store of firewood, and nightlong the fires are fed and scatter their radiance; and do men doubt to plant and lavish their care? Why should I keep by larger trees? the osier and the low broom, even they yield leafage to the herd or shade to the herdsman, and hedge the crops and pasture the honey-bee. And fain would I gaze on Cytorus billowy with boxwood, or groves of Narycian pine; fain see fields that owe no debt to the mattock nor to any mortal care. Even fruitless forests on a Caucasian summit, which angry east winds perpetually shatter and toss, yield produce after their kind, yield profit of timber, pines for ships, cedar and cypress for dwellings; from one the countryfolk turn spokes for wheels, from one fashion drum-heads for wagons and curving keels of ships; withies grow thick on osiers, leaves on elms, but strong spear-shafts on the myrtle and the cornel trusty in battle; the Ituraean yew is bent into bows; therewithal smooth lime and polished boxwood take shape under the lathe or are hollowed out by the sharp chisel; and therewithal the light alder, sent down the Po, swims on the bubbling wave; and therewithal the bees hide their swarms in the hollow bark or the core of a mouldering ilex. What have Bacchus' gifts bestowed of equal renown? Bacchus gives cause for blame likewise; he it was who laid the mad Centaurs low in death, Rhoetus and Pholus, and Hylaeus as he aimed that great flagon at the Lapithae.

Ah too fortunate the husbandmen, did they know their own felicity! on whom far from the clash of arms Earth their most just mistress lavishes from the soil a plenteous sustenance. Though no high proud-portalled house pours forth the vast tide of morning visitants that fill her halls; though they feed no gaze on doors inlaid with lovely tortoise-shell or raiment tricked out with gold or bronzes of Ephyre; though the fleece's whiteness is not stained with Assyrian dye nor the clear olive-oil spoiled for use with cinnamon; but careless quiet and life ignorant of disappointment, wealthy in manifold riches, but the peace of broad lands, caverns and living lakes, and cool pleasances and the lowing of oxen and soft slumbers beneath the tree fail not there; there are the glades and covers of game, and youth hardy in toil and trained to simplicity, divine worship and reverend age; among them justice set her last footprints as she passed away from earth.

Me indeed first and before all things may the sweet Muses, whose priest I am and whose great love hath smitten me, take to themselves and show me the pathways of the sky, the stars, and the diverse eclipses of the sun and the moon's travails; whence is the earthquake; by what force the seas swell high over their burst barriers and sink back into themselves again; why winter suns so hasten to dip in Ocean, or what hindrance keeps back the lingering nights. But if I may not so attain to this side of nature for the clog of chilly blood about my heart, may the country and the streams that water the valleys content me, and lost to fame let me love stream and woodland. Ah, where the plains spread by Spercheus, and Laconian girls revel on Taygetus! ah for one to lay me in Haemus' cool dells and cover me in immeasurable shade of boughs! Happy he who hath availed to know the causes of things, and hath laid all fears and immitigable Fate and the roar of hungry Acheron under his feet; yet he no less is blessed, who knows the gods of the country, Pan and old Silvanus and the Nymphs' sisterhood. Him fasces of the people or purple of kings sway not, not maddening discord among treacherous brethren, nor the Dacian swarming down from the leagued Danube, not the Roman state or realms destined to decay; nor may pity of the poor or envy of the rich cost him a pang. What fruits the boughs, what the gracious fields bear of their own free will, these he gathers, and sees not the iron of justice or the mad forum and the archives of the people. Others vex blind seaways with their oars, or rush upon the sword, pierce the courts and chambers of kings; one aims destruction at the city and her wretched homes, that he may drink from gems and sleep on Tyrian scarlet; another heaps up wealth and broods over buried gold; one hangs rapt in amaze before the Rostra; one the applause of populace and senate re-echoing again over the theatre carries open-mouthed away: joyfully they steep themselves in blood of their brethren, and exchange for exile the dear thresholds of their homes, and seek a country spread under an alien sun. The husbandman sunders the soil with curving plough; from this is the labour of his year, from this the sustenance of his native land and his little grandchildren, of his herds of oxen and his faithful bullocks; and unceasingly the year lavishes fruit or young of the flock or sheaf of the corn-blade, and loads the furrow and overflows the granary with increase. Winter is come; the Sicyonian berry is crushed in the olive-presses, the swine come home sleek from their acorns, the woodland yields her arbute-clusters, and autumn drops his manifold fruitage, and high up the mellow vintage ripens on the sunny rock. Meanwhile sweet children cling round his kisses, the home abides in sacred purity, the kine droop their milky udders, and on the shining grass fat kids wrestle with confronting horns. Himself keeps holiday, and stretched on the sward where the fire is in the midmost and the company wreathe the wine-bowl, calls on thee, god of the winepress, in libation, and marks an elm for contests of the flying javelin among the keepers of the flock, or they strip their hardy limbs for the rustic wrestling-match. This life the ancient Sabines kept long ago, this Remus and his brother; even thus

Etruria waxed mighty, ay, and Rome grew fairest of the world and ringed her sevenfold fortresses with a single wall. Yes, before the sceptre of that Cretan king, before a guilty race slew oxen for the banquet, this life golden Saturn led on earth; nor yet withal had they heard war-trumpets blown, nor yet the hard anvil clink under the sword.

But we have crossed a boundless breadth of plain, and now is time to loosen the necks of our steaming horses.

BOOK THIRD

THEE also, mighty Pales, and thee will we sing, O renowned shepherd of Amphrysus, and you, Lycaean woods and rivers. All else that might have held idle minds fast in song is staled by usage now: who knows not cruel Eurystheus or accursed Busiris' altars? to whom is untold the boy Hylas, and Latona in Delos, and Hippodame, or the hero of the ivory shoulder, the keen horseman Pelops? A path must be adventured where I too may rise from earth and fly triumphing on the lips of men. First will I lead home with me, if life but last, the Muses from their Aonian hill; first, my Mantua, bring thee back the palms of Idume, and build a shrine of marble on the green meadow by the waterside, where broad Mincius wanders in slow windings, and borders his banks with delicate reed. In the midst shall Caesar be my temple's habitant: to him will I, splendid in Tyrian scarlet, drive in triumph by the river an hundred chariots fourfold-yoked; for me all Greece, leaving Alpheus and the groves of Molorchus, shall contend in the foot-race or with the raw hide boxing-glove. Myself, chapleted with stripped leaves of olive, I will bear offerings: even now is it good to lead the fitly ordered processions to the shrines and see the oxen sacrificed, or the stage opening as the scenes swing round, and the inwoven Britons rising on the crimson curtains. On the doors I will fashion in gold and solid ivory the tribes of the Ganges in battle and Quirinus' conquering arms, and here Nile surging in war with swollen flood, and columns rising decked with the bronze of ships; and beside them, vanquished Asian cities and Niphates driven in rout, and the Parthian confident in flight and in his arrows shot backward, and the double trophy torn in fight from a diverse foe, and the nations twice triumphed over from either shore. There too shall stand breathing images in Parian stone, the brood of Assaracus and the names of the nation of Jove's descent, and Tros their ancestor, and the Cynthian founder of Troy: and wretched Envy shall fear the Furies and Cocytus' relentless river, the twisted serpents of Ixion, the awful wheel and the stone that never may scale the steep. Meanwhile follow we the woodland ways and fresh lawns of the wood-nymphs; thine, Maecenas, are no light commands. Without thee my spirit never springs aloft; lo, up! break off dull delay! with ringing cries Cithaeron summons, and Taygetus with his hounds and Epidaurus trainer of steeds, and the call echoes back redoubled from the applauding woods. Yet soon will I gird myself to tell of Caesar's fiery battles, and carry his name's renown through as many years as separate Caesar from Tithonus' primal birth.

Whoso either breeds horses for the wondered prize of Olympian palm, or strong bullocks for the plough, let his foremost choice be of the mothers of the herd. The best cow is ugly-shapen; her head coarse, her neck of the largest, with dewlaps hanging down from chin to leg; and to her length of flank there is no limit; large of limb and of foot, and with shaggy ears under inward-curving horns. Nor would I quarrel with one marked with spots of white, or one reluctant to the yoke and sometimes hasty with her horn, and almost like a bull to view, and tall all her length, with a tail that sweeps her footprints below her as she moves. The age for just marriage and travail of birth ceases before the tenth, begins after the fourth year. Beyond these, she is neither fit for breeding nor strong for the plough; between them, while the lusty youth of thy flock endures, let loose the males, put thy herds early to breeding, and generation by generation keep up the succession of thy stock. In this poor mortal life the fairest day is ever the first to fly; sickness and melancholy age advance, and toil and hard death's pitilessness sweep us away. Ever will there be some stock that thou wouldst exchange: then ever replace them, and that thou miss not the lost, be beforehand in selecting the young of the herd year by year.

Even in like wise must the breed of horses too be chosen: only do thou, on such as thou purposest to nurture for the hope of the race, lavish from infancy onward thy foremost pains. From the first, a well-bred foal in the fields lifts a higher pace and plants a lighter limb; he dares to advance in front and to try the threatening torrent, and trust the unknown bridge, and starts not at vain noises: his are a high crest and fine head, a short belly and fleshy back, and a breast rippling in proud slopes of muscle. Bays and greys are proper, the worst coloured are white and dun. Moreover, if haply armour clashes near, he may not stand still, he pricks his ears and quivers in all his limbs, and rolls from his nostrils a gathered volume of fiery breath. His mane is thick, and when flung up falls back on the right shoulder: a double ridge runs between his loins, and his hoof of solid horn prints the sod with heavy clatter. Such was that Cyllarus who obeyed Amyclean Pollux' rein, and the two-yoked steeds of Mars chronicled of Grecian poets, and mighty Achilles' team: such too tireless Saturn's self when, shaking the horse-mane free over his neck at his consort's coming, he filled high Pelion with his shrill neighing as he fled.

Even him, when failing either from weight of sickness or dulness of growing years, house out of sight and be not over-tender with the faults of age. Age is cold to love, and vainly drags on the ungrateful task, and when the battle is come, as it were a fire blazing without strength among stubble, he rages to no avail. Therefore spirit and youth thou wilt mark beyond all; then his other merits, his parents' breeding, and his own grief at defeat and exultation in victory. Seest thou not when in headlong contest chariots shoot into the racecourse and pour streaming from the barrier, when the young drivers' hopes are at height, and throbbing fear drains their riotous hearts? they ply the curling lash and stoop loose over the rein; the glowing axle flies fiercely on; and now they sink, and now rising high they seem to bound through empty air and mount into the wind: no slackening no r stay; the sand rises in a yellow cloud, and they are wetted by the foam and breath of the pursuers; so great is desire of honour, so great their care for victory. First Erichthonius dared to yoke four steeds to the chariot and stand triumphant rushing above the wheels; the Pelethronian Lapithae mounted on horseback and bequeathed the bridle and the ring, and taught the armed rider to spurn the sod and gather his feet proudly in the canter. For both the task is alike, alike the trainer searches out one in his prime, hot of spirit and fleet of pace, how often soever another have driven the flying foe in rout, and boast Epirus or valiant Mycenae for his country, and trace his line from Neptune's own ancestry.

Which things regarded, they are busier as the time draws near, and lavish all their care to fill out with firm fat him whom they have chosen leader and named bridegroom of the herd; and mow flowering grass and supply river-water and corn, lest he fail of mastery in the delicious toil, and ill-fed fathers have their record in weakling sons. The brood mares moreover they purposely starve into leanness, and when the foreknown pleasure stirs them first -to union, deny them the boughs and fence them from the fountain, and often shake them with galloping and tire them in the sun, while the threshing-floor groans daily under the corn-flail, and while the empty chaff flutters to the freshening west wind. This they do, that the fruitful field be not dulled. for use and the sluggish furrows choked by overabundant case, but thirstily swallow the seed and hide it deeper within.

Again the care, of the sires begins to drop and of the dams to follow in turn. When the breeding mares wander at the months' fulfilment, let no one allow them to draw heavy wagon-yokes, nor clear the road at a leap and dart over the meadows in violent speed or swim in rushing rivers. On clear lawns they feed them and beside brimming streams, where moss grows and the grass is greenest on the bank, by sheltering caves and jutting shadow of cliffs. About the groves of Silarus and Alburnus evergreen with ilex there swarms a fly whose Roman name is asilus, oestrus the Greeks render it in their speech, fierce, shrill of note, that scatters whole herds distracted through the forest: their bellowings madden the shaken air and the woods and the parched Tanager's bank. With this plague Juno of old wreaked the terrors of her wrath and counselled woe on the heifer-daughter of Inachus: this likewise, for it attacks more fiercely in the burning noons, thou shalt ward off from the breeding flock, and pasture thy herds when the sun is newly risen or the stars usher in the night.

After birth all the care passes to the calves in turn; and immediately they brand the name and mark of race on such as they choose to rear for stock-breeding, or to keep sacred for the altar, or to cleave the soil and upturn the broken clods of the ridgy meadow. The rest of the herd are at pasture on the grassy green; such as thou wilt shape to pursuit and profit of husbandry, instruct while yet ungrown, and set on the road of training while their minds are light in youth and their age flexible. And first tie round their shoulders loose rings of light osier: next, when the free neck is grown used to bondage, yoke matched bullocks in pairs by these same collars, and make them keep step each with each; and now let empty carts be often drawn by them along the ground and score a light track on the dust: thereafter may the beechen axle creak to the strain of a weighty load, and the brazen shaft pull the harnessed wheels. Meanwhile for their unbroken youth thou shalt cut not grass alone nor thin willow-leaves and marsh sedge, but the corn sown by thine hand; nor shall the mother cows after ancient use fill the snowy milking-pails, but spend all their udders on their darling children.

But if thy desire be rather towards wars and fiery squadrons, or to roll charioted by Pisa's Alphean streams and urge the flying team in the grove of Jupiter, the charger's first task is to look on warriors in pride of arms and endure the bugle note, and stand the scream of the dragging wheel and hear the rattle of harness in the stall; then more and more to rejoice in a kind word of praise from the trainer and love the sound when his neck is patted. And venturing this even when just weaned from his mother, again in turn let him yield his mouth to the soft halter, while weak and yet unsteady and yet ignorant in youth. But when three summers are past and the fourth is added, presently he may begin to pace the ring and mark time with clattering footfall, and bend his legs in alternating curves, and take the look of work; then, then let him race against the gale, and flying over open spaces, as though free from the rein, hardly lay his foot-prints on the soil's surface: even as, when the gathered North wind swoops down from Hyberborean borders and scatters the wintry and waterless clouds of Scythia, the deep cornfields and floating plains shiver in light gusts, and the forest tops utter a cry and the long waves race to the beach; he wings his way, sweeping field and flood in his level flight. Hence shall he either sweat towards Elean goals over long spaces of the course with mouth spurting bloody foam, or his supple neck better bear on the Belgic car. Then at last when now they are broken, let their body fill out with coarse mash; for before breaking their pride will swell high, and they will refuse when taken in hand to endure the tough lash and obey the cruel curb.

But no diligence more confirms their strength than to keep love and the stings of blind passion aloof, whether profit of oxen or of horses be more to our mind. And therefore they banish the bull far into lonely pasturage, behind a mountain barrier and across broad streams, or keep him shut indoors by the rich farmyard; for the female gradually wastes his strength and consumes him in gazing and allows him not to remember woodland or meadow; yes and often her sweet allurements drive her proud lovers to let their horns decide the rivalry. On broad Sila gazes the shapely heifer: they join in violent battle and alternate the frequent wound; dark blood bathes their bodies and their crashing horns strain in confronting pressure, while forest and far-stretching sky echo back. Nor will the warriors herd together; but the conquered retires, and keeps exile afar in strange regions, making many a moan over his disgrace and the haughty, conqueror's blows and his love's loss unavenged; and gazing on the stall he quits his ancestral realm. Therefore with all diligence he trains his strength and lies tireless on an unstrewn couch among flinty rocks, feeding on prickly leaves and sharp rushes; and tries himself, and learns to throw his rage into his horns by butting at a tree trunk, and buffets the winds with blows, and scatters the sand in rehearsal of battle. Thereafter, in gathered might and strength renewed, he advances his standard and rushes headlong on his forgetful foe: as a billow beginning to whiten in mid ocean gathers a lengthening curve from the deep, and as rolling landward it thunders over the rocks and falls in very mountain mass, while the wave boils up eddying from the bottom and hurls the black shingle high up the beach.

Yes all on earth, the race of man and beast, the tribes of the sea, cattle and coloured birds break into fury and fire; in all love is the same. At none other season does the lioness forgetful of her whelps range fiercer on the plains, nor the clumsy bear deal so many a death and such widespread devastation through the forests. Then the wild boar is fierce, then the tigress most fell: ah, ill is it then to stray in the solitary Libyan land! Seest thou not the shudder that thrills the whole body of the horse, if only the familiar scent is wafted on the gale? and now neither reins nor cruel whips of men, not cliffs or caverned rocks delay him, nor barring rivers that unseat and whirl away mountains with their wave. The great Sabellian boar charges with whetted tusks, tramples the earth before him and chafes his flanks on a tree, and on this side and that hardens his shoulders against wounds. What of the youth, through whose frame unrelenting love darts his mastering fire? late in the blind night be swims the straits vexed by stormy gusts, and over him thunders the mighty gate of heaven, and the seas dash echoing on the crags; nor can his wretched parents call him back, nor the maiden left with cruel death for her doom. What of Bacchus' dappled lynxes, and the fierce tribe of wolves and bounds? what of the battles fought by unwarlike deer? Doubtless before all the madness of mares is eminent, and Venus' very self inspired them on the day when that Potnian chariot-team champed the limbs of Glaucus in their jaws. Across Gargarus and across the roaring Ascanius love leads them; they scale the mountain and swim the river. And all at once when their inward longing kindles into flame, (in spring the rather, since in spring their vital heat returns,) they all wheel and stand facing the West on rocky heights, and snuff the light breezes, and often without bodily union, wind-impregned, wonderful to tell, over crag and cliff and deep-sunken vale they scatter in flight not to thy springs, O East, nor to the rising of the sun, but towards the north and northwest winds, or whence the South issues wrapped in gloom and saddens heaven with his chilly rains. Then that clammy fluid, rightly named hippomanes in shepherds' language, oozes from their groin: the hippomanes that wicked stepmothers often gather, and mingle with herbs and baleful spells.

But time fleets meanwhile, fleets beyond recovery, while in loving enthralment we pass on and on. Enough now of cattle: half of our charge is left, the herding of fleecy flocks and rough she-goats. Here is work; hence look for praise, sturdy tillers of the soil. Nor am I of doubtful mind how hard it is to win all this in words, and crown things so slight with honour. But in fond desire I am rapt over Parnassus' lonely steeps, fain to pass along the hill where the trace of no earlier wheel winds down the soft slope to Castaly.

Now, august Pales, now must sound an ampler tone. In the beginning I ordain that sheep crop their fodder in the soft pens while leafy summer lingers on his return, and that the hard ground be strewn beneath them with abundant straw and trusses of fern, lest chill frost hurt the tender flock, and bring mange or rotting feet. Thence I pass on and order for the goats store of arbute-sprays and supply of fresh river-water, and wind-sheltered pens turned to the mid-day and facing the winter sun, even when chill Aquarius is now setting showerful upon the verge of the dying year. Them too must we guard with no lighter carefulness: nor will the profit be less, how great a price soever be exchanged for Milesian fleeces steeped in Tyrian crimsons: from them is a more numerous breed, from them wealth of abundant milk; the fuller the pails have foamed from their drained udders, the richer will drip the stream when the teats are squeezed anew. And no less withal men shear the beards and silvered chins of the Cinyphian he-goat, and his hairy bristles, for service of the camp and sailcloth for hapless seafarers. Their pasture indeed is on Lycaean wood and hill-top, rough briars and brushwood clinging to the steep; and unherded they return heedfully home, leading their young, and hardly lift their heavy udders through the doorway. Therefore with all diligence, as their need of human care is the less, wilt thou guard them from frost and snowy winds, and cheerfully deal them sustenance and fodder of boughs, and keep thine hay-lofts unlocked all mid-winter. But indeed when western breezes call, and glad summer sends forth either flock into lawn and mead, with the glimmer of the morning star let us haste to the chilly countryside while morning is fresh and the grass frosty-white, and the dew on the tender herbage sweetest to the cattle. Thereafter, when the fourth hour in heaven has gathered thirst and the note of the shrill tree-crickets pierces the copses, by wells or by deep pools I will bid the flocks drink the wave that runs in troughs of ilex; but in the noonday beats seek some shady dell, where Jove's great oak, massy and old, stretches his giant boughs, or where, dark with many an ilex, broods the sacred shadow of the grove: then once more offer them the thin runlets and feed them once more about set of sun, when cool evening allays the air and now the dewy moonlight revives the lawns, and the kingfisher is loud on the shore and the warbler in the thickets.

Why pursue to thee in verse the shepherds of Libya, why their pastures and the scattered roofs of the huts that are their home? Often daylong and nightlong and the whole month unbroken the, flock goes grazing for lonely leagues without a dwelling; so wide stretches the plain. The African herdsman carries with him all his wealth, his house and household god, his weapons and Amyclaean dog and Cretan quiver; even as the valiant Roman in his ancestral arms, when he speeds his march beneath a cruel burden, and the column halts and the camp is pitched beside the surprised foe.

But not so where the tribes of Scythia border the Maeotic wave and the yellow Danube rolls thick with sand, or where outstretched Rhodope runs back under the mid pole. There they keep their herds shut in stall, and no grass shows on the plain or leaf on the tree; but earth lies featureless in mounded snow and deep fields of ice that rise to seven fathoms, under eternal winter and eternal breath of icy north-west winds. Nor ever does the sun pierce that pallid gloom, neither when he rides his horses up the steep of sky nor when he slakes his headlong chariot in Ocean's ruddy floor. Sudden ice-flakes gather on the running stream, and even now the water bears iron-tired wheels on its back, and gives broad wagons the harbourage it gave to ships before. Brass vessels burst continually, and clothes stiffen on the body, and liquid wine is cut with hatchets; whole pools turn into solid ice, and the rough icicle congeals on the shaggy beard. Meanwhile all the air is a single drift of snow: the cattle die, the broad-backed oxen stand in a frosty shroud, and the deer huddle in troops, benumbed by the fresh masses that their antler tips barely outreach. On them men slip not the hounds, hunt them not with any nets or the terror of crimson-feathered toils; but while they vainly push against the breasting hill, slay them steel in hand and cut them down deep-braying and with merry clamour carry them home. Themselves in caverns deep sunken under earth they fleet their careless leisure, and roll to the hearth oak from the wood-pile and whole elms to feed the fire. Here they pass the night in games, and with beer and bitter meaths joyously counterfeit draughts of the vine. Such is the wild race of men that lies under the seven stars of the utmost North, buffeted by Rhipaean gales and wrapped in the tawny fur of beasts.

If wool-growing be thy care, first keep far from brushwood, from bur and briar; shun rank pasturage; and choose from the beginning a white and soft-fleeced flock. The ram moreover, be he else silvery as may be, if only his tongue is black under the moist palate, reject thou, or he will darken the lamb's fleeces with dusky spots, and choose another from the flock that fills the meadow. With such snowy wool for dower, if belief be deigned, Pan the god of Arcady ensnared thee, O Moon, in his treachery, when he called thee into the depth of woodland and thou didst not scorn his call.

But whoso sets his heart on milk, let him with his own hand carry store of lucerne and lotus, and salted grass to the pens: so they desire water the more, and the more swell their udders, and give back in the milk an undertaste of salt. Many too take the new-born kids from their mothers, and fix iron-spiked muzzles on their baby mouths. What they milk at dayspring or in the daylight hours, they let curdle at night; what at gathering dusk and with the setting sun, they pack off in frails at dawn and the shepherd trudges to the town; or sprinkle it sparingly with salt and store it up for winter.

Neither be the care of thy dogs the last-deferred; but feed together on fattening whey the puppies of the fleet Spartan and the keen Molossian: never in their guard shalt thou dread thief by night in thy pens or inroad of wolves or restless Iberians behind thee; often likewise wilt thou urge the chase of the shy wild ass, and course hare or fallow deer with thy hounds, often rout the boar startled with their baying from his woodland wallowing-pool, and high among the hills drive the lordly stag with shouts into thy nets.

Learn also to burn scented cedar in the stalls, and clear out noisome scaled snakes with fumes of gum. Often under sheds long unmoved the dangerous viper lurks and shrinks fearfully out of the daylight; or that sore plague of oxen, wont to glide under the shadow of the roof and dart his venom at the flock, the snake lodges in the ground. Snatch up sticks and stones, O shepherd, and as he rises threatening and puffs out his hissing throat, strike him down! and now he hides his head deep in fearful flight, while his coiling body and the last folds of his tail unwind, and he slowly trails the utmost curve of his rings. Likewise there is that malign serpent of Calabrian lawns that rolls along with uplifted breast, scaly-backed and marked with large spots down the length of his belly; who while streams yet gush from their fountain-heads, and while earth is wet with moist spring and southern rains, lives in ponds and housing on river banks, there greedily fills his black gorge with fish and chattering frogs; after the marsh is burnt up and the earth cracks in the blazing sun, he darts out over the dry land and rages in the fields, rolling his fiery eyes, exasperate in thirst and frantic with heat. May I not then be tempted to take soft sleep beneath the sky, or lie along the grass on the forest ridge, when fresh from his cast slough and glittering in youth he glides forth stately in the sunlight, leaving his young or his eggs at home, and his mouth flickers with triple-forked tongue.

Likewise will I instruct thee of diseases in their sources and signs. Rotting mange attacks sheep when icy rains and the hoar frost of rough mid-winter sink deep in their live flesh, or when, after shearing, the sweat clots unwashed and tangled brairs cut their body. Therefore the keepers bathe all the flock in fresh running water, and the ram is plunged in the pool and sent floating down stream with drenched fleece: or they smear the shorn bodies with bitter olive-lees, and mingle scum of silver and virgin sulphur, pitch of Ida and wax ointment, and squills and strong-smelling hellebore and black asphalt. Yet no device helps the trouble more, than when one can cut away the festering surface with steel; the sore is fed into life by conceal-ment while the shepherd refuses to lay healing hands to the wound and sits idly praying to his gods for better fortune. Nay, and when raging pains run deep in the bleating people and parching fever preys on their limbs, it is found of service to allay the burning heat and strike a vein where it throbs with blood between the hoofs: as is the wonted manner of Bisaltae, or of the fierce Gelonian in retreat to Rhodope and Getan solitudes, whose drink is milk curdled with blood of mares. If from far thou seest one passing oftener into the languid shade, or more listlessly cropping the tops of grass and following behind the rest, or lying down in mid-pasture of the meadow and retiring alone before deepening night, straightway check the evil with thy knife ere the terrible infection spread, through the heedless multitude. Not so heavy comes the rush of rain when a squall sweeps over the sea as diseases multiply in the flock: neither do ailments seize them singly, but whole summer-pastures at a stroke, the flock and the flock's hope together, and all the race root and branch; as any may know who sees even now so long afterward, by soaring Alps and Noric hill-forts and fields of Iapydian Timavus, the deserted pastoral realm and far-stretching lawns left desolate.

Here once the air sickened and a woful season came, that kindling with the gathered heat of autumn dealt death on all the tribes of cattle and wild beasts, and poisoned the rotting pools and putrid fodder. Nor was the march of death straight forward: but when fiery thirst coursing in all the veins had shrunk the aching limbs, again the watery humours flooded out and all the bones dissolving under the disease melted into them piecemeal. Often amid divine sacrifice the victim standing by the altar, while the snowy-ribboned fillet of wool was being twined about it, fell dying among the tardy ministrants. Or had the priestly steel slain in time, no flame rises from those filaments when laid upon the altar, nor can the soothsayer return counsel or reply: hardly is the knife at the throat stained by the blood or the sand's surface darkened by the thin gore. Next calves lie dying all over the luxuriant grass, and yield up their sweet life by the full manger: next madness comes on the kindly dogs, and a hard rattling cough and choking swelling of the throat on the sickened swine. Joyless in his exercises and heedless of the grass the victor steed pines, and turns away from the fountain, and beats the earth with impatient foot: his ears droop, and by them sweat comes and goes, and that cold and betokening death: his skin is dry and hard when stroked, and resists the touch. Such are the signs that for the first days foreshadow the end; but as the sickness begins to advance and gather violence, then indeed their eyes burn and their breath is fetched deep, heavy with broken moans, their flanks below heave with long-drawn sobs, black blood oozes from their nostrils, and their throat is blocked by their rough and swollen tongue. It helped to thrust in a horn and pour down it juice of the winepress; that seemed the one restorative for the dying: in short space the very cure was fatal; reviving they maddened in fever. and even in mortal weakness (the gods send better things to the righteous and that bewilderment on our foes!) they tore and mangled their own limbs with naked teeth. And lo, smoking under the iron share the bull drops down, spurts from his mouth mingled blood and foam, and heaves a last groan: sadly the ploughman advancing unyokes the bullock mourning his brother's death and leaves the plough stuck fast in mid-furrow. Not shades of stately groves, not soft meadows can stir his sense, not the river that curls brighter than amber over his rocks to seek the plain; but his deep flanks relax, his dull eyes are weighed down in stupor, and his neck sinks drooping heavily to earth. What avails his toil or services? what that his ploughshare has upturned the ponderous clods? And yet no Massic bounty of the vine, no crowding banquets have done harm to these; they feed on leaves and simple pasture of grass, their cups are clear springs and racing rivers, nor does care break their healthful sleep. Then as never before they say that in that countryside oxen were to seek for Juno's rites, and chariots were drawn by ill-matched buffaloes to the high votive shrines. Therefore they wearily furrow earth with mattocks, and cover in the seed-corn with their own nails, and with straining necks drag their creaking wagons over the hill heights. No more does the wolf prowl in ambush round the sheepfolds nor pace nightlong nigh the flocks; a fiercer care makes him tame. Shy fallow deer and timid stags now stray among the dogs and about the houses. Nay the brood of the infinite sea and all the tribe of swimming creatures lie on the verge of the strand like shipwrecked corpses in the wash of the wave, and seals take unwonted refuge in the river: and in the vain defence of her winding recesses the viper perishes, and the snake with scales stiffened in dismay: to the very birds the air is cruel, and they drop, leaving their life high under the clouds. Furthermore, no change of food is now aught of avail, and arts are sought but for harm; Chiron son of Phillyra and Amythaonian Melampus give up their mastery. Loosed into daylight from Stygian gloom wan Tisiphone maddens, and drives plague and panic before her, and day by day towers insatiate with higher uplifted head; river and parched bank and couchant hill echo with incessant lowings and bleating of flocks. And now she deals destruction in battalions, and heaps the very folds with carcases rotting in foul decay, till men learn to cover them with earth and hide them out of sight in pits. For neither might the hides be used nor can any one dissolve or consume the flesh in water or flame: not even can they shear the fleeces, eaten through by corruption of the pestilence, nor set hand to the rotten web: nay, even if any had braved so abhorred a garment burning pustules and foul-smelling sweat overran his limbs, and in no long space of delay thereafter the fatal fire devoured his infected frame.

BOOK FOURTH

NEXT will I advance to heaven-born honey, the gift of air, (let this likewise, Maecenas, share thy regard,) and tell thee of the wondrous show of a tiny state, of high-hearted princes, and a whole nation's ordered works and ways, tribes and battles. Slight is the field of labour; but not slight the glory, if but thwarting deities allow, and Apollo listen to prayer.

First of all a home must be sought for bees, and a post where neither winds may have entry--for winds hinder them carrying their forage home--nor sheep and butting kids tread down the flowers, or the straying heifer brush the dew from the meadow and trample the springing grass. Likewise let the bright scale-backed lizard be far from their rich folds, and the birds that come with the bee-eater, and the swallow, her breast marked with those blood-stained hands: for they spread universal havoc, and carry off the bees on the wing, dainty morsels for their fierce nestlings. But let clear springs be nigh, and ponds green with moss, and a thread of rill fleeting through the grass; and let a palm or tall wild-olive overshadow the entrance, that when the new kings shall lead forth their earliest swarms in the sweet springtime, and the young brood disport unprisoned from the comb, the bordering bank may woo them to cool retreat, and the tree meet and stay them in her leafy shelter. Amid the water, whether it stagnate or run, cast large stones and willow-boughs crosswise, that they may have many a bridge to stand on and spread their wings to the summer sun if haply a shower overtake them or a gust of wind plunge them in the watery realm. All round green casia and far-fragrant wild thyme and wealth of heavy-scented savory should bloom, and violet beds drink the channelled spring. Let thy hives moreover, whether they be stitched of hollow bark or woven from pliant osier, have narrow doorways; for the honey freezes in winter cold, and again melts and wastes in the heat. Extreme of either the bees dread alike; nor in vain do they eagerly plaster with wax the draughty chinks in the roof and stop up the rims with pollen of flowers, and for this very service gather and store their gum, stickier than bird-lime or pitch from Phrygian Ida. Often likewise, if the tale is true, they keep house in recesses scooped out underground, or are found deep in hollow sandstone or the cavern of a mouldering tree. Yet do thou smear smooth clay warmly round about their creviced chambers, and spread on the top a thin coat of leaves. Neither suffer the yew too near their house, neither burn crab-shells to redness in the fire, neither trust them where a marsh is deep or by a strong smell of mire, or where encircling rocks echo to a stroke and fling back the phantom of a call.

For the rest, when the golden sun has driven winter routed underground and flung wide the sky in summer light, forthwith they range over lawn and wood, and harvest the shining blossoms and sip lightly of the streams; then glad with some strange delight, they nurture their brood in the nest, then deftly forge the fresh wax and mould the clammy honey. Then, as looking up thou seest their armies swarming skyward from the hives and floating through the clear summer air, and wonderest at their dim cloud trailing in the wind, mark! ever they steer for sweet water and leafy shelter. Here sprinkle the odours ordained, crushed balm and lowly tufts of honeywort, and make a tinkling round about and clash the cymbals of our Lady; themselves will settle on the scented seat, themselves in their wonted way creep into the inmost covert of their nest.

But further, if they are gone forth to battle-for often high swelling discord rises between two kings, and at once and afar thou mayest foreknow the raging of the multitude and the hearts beating fast for war; for a note as of the hoarse brass of our Mars chides the lingerers and a cry is heard that mimics broken trumpet-blasts:--then they muster hurriedly together with vibrating wings, and whet their stings on their beaks and brace their arms, and crowd in mingled mass round their king and close up to the royal tent, and with loud cries challenge the enemy. So when they find the spring sky rainless and their field open, they sally from the gates; high in air the armies clash and the din swells; gathering they cluster in a great ball and come tumbling down, thick as hailstones through the air or the rain of acorns from the shaken ilex. The monarchs move splendid-winged amid the ranks, and mighty passions stir in their tiny breasts, stubborn to the last not to retreat, till weight of the conqueror forces these or those to turn backward in flying rout. These stormy passions and these mighty conflicts will be lulled to rest by a handful of scattered dust.

But when thou hast recalled both leaders from the battlefield, do to death him who seems inferior, that he be not a waste and barm; let the better reign in a clear court. One will be ablaze with spots of embossed gold; for there are two kinds, this the better, fair of feature and splendid in flashing scales; the other, rough-coated and sluggish, crawls meanly with his breadth of belly. As the two kings in aspect so are their subjects shapen; for some are rough and dirty, even as a traveller when he issues from deep dust and spits from his mouth the gritty soil, all athirst; others shine and sparkle in splendour, and their bodies blaze with evenly marked drops of gold. These are the choicer breeds; from their combs at the ordained season of the skies thou shalt squeeze sweet honey, and yet less sweet than crystal-clear, to soften the harsh taste of wine.

But when the swarms fly aimlessly at play in the sky, and despise their combs and leave their house to grow cold, thou shalt stop their light-minded and idle game. Nor is it much work to stop; tear off the wings of the kings; while they linger, not a bee will dare to set out on their aëry way or move standard from the camp. Let garden plots woo them with fragrance of their yellow flowers, and the watchman of thieves and birds, Hellespontic Priapus, keep them in guard with his hook of willow. Himself should the keeper of such plant about their houses broad belts of thyme and laurels brought from the hill heights; himself wear his hand hard with work, himself bed the soil with fruitful shoots and water them with kindly showers.

And truly, but that already nearing my task's final limit I furl my sails and hasten to turn my prow to land, perchance I might also sing of the care and keeping that deck the rich garden mould, and of the Paestan rosebeds with their double blossoming, and how the endive rejoices in drinking the rill and the banks are green with parsley, and how the curved gourd swells bellying along the grass, nor had kept silence of the late-flowering narcissus or the shoot of the curled acanthus and pale ivy-sprays and the myrtles that love the shore. For I remember how beneath the towered fortress of Oebalia, where dark Galaesus moistens his golden cornfields, I saw an old man of Corycus, who owned some few acres of waste land, a field neither rich for grazing nor favourable to the flock nor apt for the vineyard; yet he, setting thinly sown garden-stuff among the brushwood, with borders of white lilies and vervain and the seeded poppy, equalled in his content the wealth of kings; and returning home when night was late, would heap his table with unbought dainties. The first roses of spring, the first apples of autumn he would gather; and when even yet the frost of bitter winter cleft the rocks and laid an icy curb on the running waters, already he plucked the soft-tressed hyacinth, chiding the late-lingering summer and the west wind's delay. So likewise was he the first for whom the bees' brood overflowed in swarming multitudes, and the frothing honey drained from the squeezed combs; lime trees were his, and wealth of pine; and as many apples as had arrayed his orchard-tree in the fresh blossom, so many it carried ripe at autumn. He too transplanted into rows full-grown elms and the hard-wood pear, and the blackthorn with sloes already upon it, and the plane already yielding shade to the drinker. But this for my part, debarred by jealous limits, I pass by and leave to be told by others after me.

Now come, I will set forth the gifts wherewith Jove himself has dowered bees at birth, their wages when, following the musical cries and tinkling brasses of the Curetes, they fed the king of heaven in that low cave of Crete. Alone they have community of children and shelter of a confederate city, and spend their life under majesty of law; alone they know a native country and established gods of the household, and, mindful of winter's coming, they ply their summer task and lay up their gatherings in a common store. For some are diligent to provide food, and labour in the fields by ordinance of the league; others within their fortified houses lay the combs' first foundations with tear of narcissus and sticky resin of bark, and hang thereon the clinging waxen walls: some guide forth the grown brood, their nation's hope; others press down the pure virgin honey and brim the cells with liquid sweets. To certain of them falls the lot of guard at the gates, and in turn they keep watch on showers and cloudy skies, or take the loads of the incomers, or in ranked array keep the drones, that idle gang, aloof from the folds: the work is all aswarm, and fragrance breathes from the thyme-scented honey. And even as when the Cyclopean forgers of the thunder hurry on the ductile ore, some make the wind come and go in bellows of bull-hide, some dip the hissing brass in the trough; Etna groans under their anvils' pressure, as alternating they lift their arms mightily in time, and turn the iron about in the grip of their tongs: even so, if small things may be compared with great, are our Attic bees urged on each in her proper duty by inborn love of possession. The aged have the town in charge, and the walling of the combs and the shaping of the curious chambers; but the younger return weary when night grows late, their thighs laden with thyme, and pasture all abroad on arbutus and grey willow, on casia and the crimsoned crocus, and the rich lime-blossom and the rust-red hyacinth. For all is one rest from toil, work-time for all is one. With morning they stream out of their gates,; nowhere a lingerer; alike again, when evening warns them at last to quit their meadow pasture, then they seek their home, then they refresh their bodies; murmuring, they hum around the edges of the doorway. Thereafter, when now they are quiet in their cells, silence deepens with night, and kindly slumber overspreads their tired limbs. Nor indeed when rain threatens do they withdraw very far from their folds, or trust the sky when cast winds are on their way; but fetch water in shelter close round their city walls, and essay short sallies, and often lift pebbles, as boats take in ballast when they rock in the tossing surge, and poise themselves so among the bodiless clouds.

This custom approved of bees may truly waken thy wonder, that they neither delight in bodily union, nor melt away in languor of love, or bear their young by birth-throes; but straight from the leaves, from the scented herbage gather their children in their mouths, themselves keep up the succession of king and tiny citizens, and fashion anew their halls and waxen realm. Often moreover in wandering they crush their wings against flinty rocks and freely yield their life beneath the burden; such is their love of flowers and their pride in honey-making. Therefore although their own life be brief and soon taken to its rest--since to the seventh summer it lasts and no further--yet the race abides immortal, and through many years the Fortune of their house stands, and their ancestors are counted to the third and fourth generation.

Furthermore not Egypt and mighty Lydia, not the Parthian peoples or the Mede by Hydaspes so adore their king. Their king safe, all are of one mind; he lost, they break allegiance, plunder the honey-cells themselves have built, and break open the plaited combs. He is guardian of their labours; him they regard, and all gather round in murmuring throng and encompass him in their swarms; and often lift him on their shoulders and shield him in war with their bodies, and seek through wounds a glorious death.

Noting this and led by these instances, certain have claimed for bees a share of some divine intelligence and a draught of the springs of heaven. For God, they say, extends through all lands and spaces of sea and depths of sky; from him flocks and herds and men and all the race of wild creatures, each at birth, draw the slender stream of life; to him thereafter all things as surely return, and are dissolved into him again; nor is there place for death; but living they flit to their starry mansions and rise to a heaven above.

If ever thou wilt unseal their imperial dwellings and the stored honey in their treasuries, first sprinkle thyself and wash thy mouth with a draught of water and hold forth searching smoke in thine hand. Twice men gather the heavy foison in two seasons of harvest: so soon as Taygete the Pleiad shows forth her august face upon the world, and spurns with her foot the recoiling ocean streams; or again when retreating before the star of the rainy Fish she sinks from a glooming sky into the wintry waves. They are furious beyond measure, and when attacked breathe venom in their bite and fastening on the veins leave their buried stings behind and lay down their lives in the wound. But if dreading a hard winter thou wilt spare future provision and compassionate their broken spirit and shattered estate, yet to fumigate with thyme and cut away the empty cells who could hesitate? for often unnoticed the eft nibbles at the combs, and beetles build their nests and hide out of the light, and the drone, sitting idle at another's board, or the fierce hornet joins battle with overpowering arms, or moths, an ill-omened tribe, or the spider hated of Minerva spreads her loose web in the doorway. The lower they are brought, the more eagerly will all press on to repair the ruin of their fallen race, and will fill their galleries and build their woven granaries of blossoms.

If indeed, since to bees also life brings such mischances as ours, they droop under sore bodily ailment;--and this thou wilt readily know by no uncertain signs: straightway their colour changes in sickness; they lose their looks and grow thin and haggard, and carry out of doors the bodies of their dead and lead the gloomy funeral train; and either hang clutching by their feet at the doorway, or shut their house and idle within, spiritless with hunger and benumbed by a cramping chill. Then a deeper hum is heard, and they murmur in long-drawn tone, like the cold south wind sighing in the forest, like the hissing waves of a restless ebbing sea, like the fierce fire roaring behind the furnace doors. Hereat I will counsel thee to burn scented gum and drip honey in through pipes of reed, calling with uninvited urgence the tired creatures to their familiar food. It will be well to mingle withal juice of pounded galls, and dry rose leaves, or wine boiled thick over a strong fire, or raisin-clusters from the Psithian vine, and Attic thyme and strong-smelling centaury. Likewise there is a meadow-flower named amellus by hus-bandmen, a plant easily found by the seeker, for it lifts from a single stalk a dense growth of shoots; golden the flower, but the petals that cluster thickly round it are dark violet shot with crimson; often the gods' altars are decked with its woven wreaths; it tastes bitter in the mouth; shepherds gather it in the cropped valley grass and beside the winding streams of Mella. Boil the roots of this in fragrant wine and set it in basketfuls for food by the doorway.

But for one whom the whole breed shall fail of a sudden, and he have nothing left to renew the race in a fresh family, it is time to unfold further the famed invention of the Arcadian keeper, and in what wise often ere now bees have been born from the putrefying blood of a slain bullock. More fully will I discover all the tale and trace it from its earliest source. For where the favoured race of Macedonian Canopus dwell by the still broad overflow of Nile and ride round their own farms in painted boats, and where the quivered Persian land presses nigh and the rushing river that pours straight down from the swarthy Indians parts into seven separate mouths and enriches green Egypt with its dark sand, all the realm builds on this art a certain remedy. First a small room is chosen, straitened down just to serve for this; they confine it by a narrow tiled roof and cramped walls, and towards the four winds add four windows with slanting lights. Then is sought a calf of two years old with horns already curving from his forehead; his double nostrils and breathing mouth are stopped up, spite of all his struggling, and he is beaten to death and the flesh pounded to pulp through the unbroken skin. Thus they leave him shut close, laying under his sides broken boughs and thyme, and fresh sprays of casia. This is done when west winds first ruffle the waters, ere yet the meadows flush with fresh colours, ere yet the chattering swallow hang her nest from the rafters. Meanwhile the humours heat and ferment in the soft bones, and creatures wonderfully fashioned may be seen, at first limbless, but soon they stir with rustling wings, and more and more drink in the delicate air: until like a shower bursting from summer clouds they swarm forth, or like arrows from the quivering bowstring when light Parthian skirmishers advance to battle.

Who, O Muses, who wrought for us this miraculous art? Whence did this strange experience enter the paths of men?

The shepherd Aristaeus fled from Peneian Tempe, his bees lost, they say, by sickness and scarcity, and stood sad by the holy spring of the river-head, and with many a complaint called thus upon her who bore him. Mother, Cyrene mother, who dwellest here deep beneath the flood, why hast thou borne me in the gods' illustrious line--if indeed my father is he whom thou sayest, Apollo of Thymbra--to be the scorn of doom? or whither is thy love for me swept away? why didst thou bid me aspire to heaven? Lo, even this mere pride of my mortal life, so hardly wrought out by infinite endeavour in skilful tendance of harvest and flock, this, and thou art my mother, I see depart. Nay come, and with thine own hand uproot my fruitful orchards, carry destroying fire into the folds and kill the harvests, wither the cornfields and wield the strong axe upon the vines, if thou art grown so weary of my praise.

But from her chamber in the river depth the mother heard his cry. Around her the Nymphs carded Milesian fleeces stained with rich sea-dyes, Drymo and Xantho, Ligea and Phyllodoce, their bright tresses falling loose over their snowy necks; and Cydippe and golden-haired Lycorias, the one a maiden, the other even then knowing the first throes of travail; and Clio and Beroë her sister, both daughters of Ocean, both decked with gold, both girt with dappled skins; arid Ephyre and Opis and Asian Deïopea, and fleet Arethusa, her arrows at last laid by. And among them Clymene was telling of Vulcan's fruitless care, and the wiles of Mars and the stolen sweetness, and recounting from Chaos downward the myriad loves of the gods. And while amid the witchery of her song the soft spun wool curls off their distaffs, again Aristaeus' lament thrilled his mother's ears, and all were motionless on their crystal chairs; but before the rest of the sisterhood Arethusa glanced forth, lifting her golden head above the wave, and cried from afar: O not vainly startled by so heavy a moan, Cyrene sister, he thine own, thy chiefest care, mourning Aristaeus stands in tears by Peneus' ancestral wave, and calls thee cruel and names thy name. To her the mother, stricken in soul with fresh alarm, Lead him, quick, lead him to us; he, she cries, may unforbidden tread the threshold of gods. With that she bids the deep streams retire, leaving a broad path for his steps to enter in. But round him the mountain-wave stood curving and clasped him in its mighty fold, and sped him beneath the river. And now marvelling at his mother's home and watery realm, cavern-locked pools and roaring forests, he passed on, and, stunned by the vast whirl of waters,, gazed on all the great floods of distant regions rolling under earth, Phasis and Lycus, and the spring bead whence breaks forth high Enipeus' source, whence the lord of Tiber and whence the streams of Anio, and Hypanis roaring over his rocks, and Mysian Caïcus and, with the twin gilded horns on his bull's forehead, Eridanus, than whom no other river flows fiercer out through his rich tilth into the shining sea. After they entered the chamber with its hanging roof of rock, and Cyrene heard her son's idle tale of tears, her sisters duly pour clear spring-water on his hands and bring towels with close-cut fleece: others pile the banquet on the board and array the brimming cups; flame of Panchaean spice swells from the altars, and his mother cries, Take up a flagon of Maeonian wine; let us pour libation to Oceanus. Herself therewithal. offers prayer to Oceanus father of all things and to the Nymphs' sisterhood who have an hundred forests, an hundred floods in their keeping: thrice she pours clear nectar over the blazing altar-fire, thrice the flame flared up anew to the crown of the roof. And strengthening his courage by this omen, she thus begins:

In the Carpathian sea-gulf dwells a soothsayer, blue Proteus, whose chariot yoked with fishes and twy-footed coursers spans the mighty ocean plain. He now visits again Emathia's borders and his birthplace of Pallene; to him we Nymphs do worship, and aged Nereus our lord; for he has the seer's knowledge of all things that are or that have been or that draw nigh to their coming: this by grace of Neptune, whose monstrous flocks and ugly seals he herds under the gulf. Him, my son, must thou first enfetter, that he may fully unfold the source of the sickness, and give prosperous issue. For without force he will give counsel in nowise, nor wilt thou bend him by entreaties; with sheer force and fetters must thou tie thy prisoner; around them his wiles at last will break unavailing. Myself will lead thee, when the sun has kindled the heat of noon, when the grass is athirst and the shade now grows more grateful to the flock, to the old man's covert, his retreat from the weary waves, that while he lies asleep thou mayest lightly assail him. But when thou shalt hold him caught and fettered in thine hands, even then the form and visage of manifold wild beasts shall cheat thee; for in a moment he will turn to a bristly boar or a black tiger, a scaly serpent and tawny-necked lioness, or will roar shrill in flame and so slip out of the fetters, or will melt into thin water and be gone. But the more be changes into endless shapes, the more do thou, my son, strain tight the grasp of his fetters, until his body change again into the likeness thou sawest when his eyes drooped and his sleep began.

So says she and sprinkles abroad liquid scent of ambrosia, anointing with it all the body of her son: but his ranged curls breathed a sweet fragrance, and supple strength grew in his limbs. There is a vast cave in the hollowed mountain side, where countless waves are driven before the gale and break among the deep recesses: of old a sure anchorage for mariners caught by storm: within it Proteus takes shelter behind the barrier of a mighty rock. Here the Nymph places her son in hiding away from the light, and herself stands apart dim in a mist. Now fierce Sirius blazed from the sky, scorching the thirsty Indian, and the fiery sun had swept to his mid arch: the grass was parched, and in hollow river-beds, dry-mouthed, the heated mud baked in his rays; when Proteus advanced from the waves to seek his familiar cavern; around him the wet tribes of the mighty deep gambolling splashed wide the briny spray. His seals stretch themselves asleep here and there along the shore; he, as some guardian of a hill-fold when evening leads the calves homeward from pasture and the wolves rouse as they hear the bleating of the lambs, takes his seat on a rock among them and tells their tale. And upon him Aristaeus, as his chance offers, hardly allowing the ancient to settle his weary limbs, darts with a loud cry and slips the shackles over him as he lies. He in return, not unmindful of his cunning, transforms himself into things manifold and marvellous, fire and dreadful wild beast and flowing river. But when none of his magic finds him escape, he returns foiled into his own shape and at length speaks with human visage: Ah, who bade thee, most venturous youth, draw nigh our home? or what wouldst thou? be cries. But be: Thou knowest, O Proteus, thyself knowest: nor canst thou at all delude me. But cease to struggle. Following divine commands we are come, to seek here oracular counsel for a worn estate. So far he spoke: thereat the soothsayer at last violently rolled the glassy orbs of his flaming eyes, and gnashing his teeth heavily thus gave voice to fate:

Not save by wrath of deity art thou plagued: great is the crime thou dost expiate. This punishment, less than deserved, wretched Orpheus calls forth upon thee--unless Fate oppose--in mad grief for his wife torn away. She indeed, flying headlong before thee through the river, saw not her death upon her in the deep grass before her girlish feet, where that monstrous snake guarded the bank. But the band of her Dryad playmates filled the mountain summits with their cries: Rhodopeïan fortresses wept, and Pangaean heights and Rhesus' martial land, Getae and Hebrus, and Actian Orithyia. He, soothing his love-sickness on his hollow shell, sang of thee, O sweet wife, of thee alone on the solitary shore, of thee at dayspring, of thee at the death of day. Even that gorge of Taenarus, the high gateway of Dis, and the grove that glooms in horror of darkness he entered, and drew nigh the ghostly people and their awful king, and the hearts that know not to melt at human supplications. But startled by his song from the deep sunken realm of Erebus thin shadows rose and phantoms of the lost to light, millionfold as birds shelter in the leaves when evenfall or wintry rain drives them from the hill; matrons and men and bodies of high-hearted heroes whose life was done, boys and unwedded girls and young men laid on the pyre before their parents' eyes: whom all round the black slime and ugly reeds of Cocytus and the sluggish wave of the unlovely pool enfetter, and Styx severs with the barrier of her ninefold flood. Nay, the very halls of death and Hell's recesses were amazed, and the Furies with livid serpents twined in their tresses; Cerberus held his triple jaws agape, and Ixion's whirling wheel hung motionless on the wind. And now his returning feet had outsped every peril, and his regained Eurydice was issuing to upper air, following at his back--for thus had Proserpine ordained--when a sudden madness seized the unwary lover, surely to be forgiven, if Death knew forgiveness. He stopped; his own Eurydice was just on the edge of daylight; forgetful, alas! and impassioned he looked round on her. There all his toil was spilt and the treaty broken with that merciless monarch; and thrice a thunder pealed over the pools of Avernus. Who, woe's me! she cries, hath destroyed me, and thee with me, Orpheus? what frenzy is this? Lo, again the cruel fates call me backward, and sleep hides my swimming eyes. And now goodbye: I pass away wrapped in a great darkness, and helplessly stretching towards thee the hands that, alas! are not thine. She spoke and suddenly out of his eyes, like vapour melting in the thin air, fled into the distance, neither saw him more as he vainly grasped at the shadows and fain would say many a word; nor did the gatekeeper of Orcus suffer him again to cross that barring pool. What could he do? or whither turn now his wife was twice torn away? how stir Death with weeping, what deities with his cry? and she even now floated cold in the Stygian bark. Seven whole months unbroken they say be wept alone beneath an aëry rock by Strymon's solitary wave, and poured forth all his tale under the freezing stars, soothing tigresses and moving oaks with song: even as the nightingale mourning under the poplar shade moans her lost brood whom the cruel ploughman has marked and torn unfledged from the nest: but she weeps nightlong, and seated on the bough renews her pitiable song and fills the region round with her mournful complaint. Never did love nor ever a bridal stir his spirit: alone he ranged Hyperborean icefields and snowy Tanaïs and Rhipaean plains that never unloose their frosts, murmuring over his lost Eurydice and the vain gifts of Dis: till slighted by such tribute, Ciconian matrons, amid divine sacrifice and Bacchic revels by night, rent him asunder and scattered him wide over the land. Even then, when torn from the marble neck his head went rolling down the mid-eddies of Oeagrian Hebrus, the very voice and chill tongue cried Eurydice! ah poor Eurydice! as their life ebbed away: Eurydice! the banks re-echoed all down the stream.

Thus Proteus, and sprang with a bound into the sea depths, and where be sprang the wave spun eddying in foam. But not so Cyrene: for she accosted him in words of cheer:

O my son, thou mayest dismiss the care that saddens thy soul. This is all the source of the sickness; this why the Nymphs with whom she wheeled the dance in depth of groves have dealt destruction on thy poor bees. Do thou humbly seek their favour with gifts outstretched, and worship the gracious maidens of the lawn: for to thy prayers they will yield pardon and relent from wrath. But first I will tell thee duly what is the way of supplication. Choose out four noble bulls of stately girth that now graze the heights of green Lycaeus, and as many heifers whose neck no yoke has touched; for these rear four altars by the lofty shrines of the goddesses and let the devoted blood trickle from their throats. and leave the bodies of the oxen alone in the leafy copse. Thereafter, when the ninth dawn brightens to her birth. thou shalt send Lethean poppies for funeral gifts to Orpheus, and adore appeased Eurydice with a slain heifer-calf, and sacrifice a black ewe and again seek the grove.

Delaying not, forthwith he fulfils his mother's counsels He comes to the shrines; he bids the ordained altars rise. four noble bulls of stately girth he leads up, and as many heifers whose neck knows not the yoke; thereafter, when the ninth dawn had risen to her birth, he sends funeral gifts to Orpheus and again seeks the grove. Here indeed they descry a portent sudden and strange to tell; bees humming among the dissolving flesh of the carcases and swarming forth from the rent sides of the oxen, and trailing in endless clouds, till now they stream together on the tree-top and hang clustering from the pliant boughs.

Thus I sang of the tending of fields and flocks and trees, while great Caesar hurled war's lightnings by high Euphrates and gave statutes among the nations in welcome supremacy, and scaled the path to heaven. Even in that season I Virgil, nurtured in sweet Parthenope, went in the flowery ways of lowly Quiet: I who once played with shepherd's songs, and in youth's hardihood sang thee, O Tityrus, under the covert of spreading beech.

www.ingramcontent.com/pod-product-compliance
Lightning Source LLC
Chambersburg PA
CBHW051553010526
44118CB00022B/2687